The Ten Unwealthy Habits

The Ten
Unwealthy Habits

Alicia Castillo Holley

Wealthing® 2011
Humble, TX

This publication contains the opinions and ideas of its author. It is intended to provide helpful and informative material on the subjects addressed in this publication. It is sold with the understanding that the publisher and the author are not engaged in rendering legal, counseling, or any other kind of personal professional services in the book. The reader should consult a competent professional for any advice if needed before adopting any of the suggestions in this book or drawing inferences from it.

The author and the publisher specifically disclaim all responsibility for any liability, loss, or risk, personal or otherwise, which is incurred as a consequence, directly or indirectly, of the use and application of any of the content of this book.

ISBN: 978-1460912614

Library of Congress Control Number 2011923141

Cover design: Goran Paunovic
Editing: Robert Geary and Carrol Strain
Interior Design: Walton Mendelson

Printed in the United States of America
Bulk purchases: danchape@wealthing.com

Publisher: Wealthing®, Humble, Tx
Wealthing® is a registered trademark.

Contents

Why Unwealthy Habits?

Most people I know are not happy with their wealth. They work very hard; they save; they read books; they try this or that; but for some reason, they are stuck. I started observing and analyzing what some of my clients and friends were doing. My theory was that they were doing the right things, while, at the same time, they were thinking and acting in ways that prevented them from achieving the desired results. By analyzing what was holding these people back, I discovered ten common habits—the ten unwealthy habits. Becoming aware of and managing these habits had a profound effect on people's wealth.

Why Unwealthy Habits

LET'S MAKE AN ANALOGY WITH HEALTH ISSUES. We all value our health. Information about being healthy abounds; we are told to exercise, eat well, not smoke, limit stress, and so on. What about looking at the habits that hold us back? What good are these healthy habits if we put ourselves at risk by not using a seat belt? Understanding and managing the habits that hold us back is as important as understanding and managing those that move us closer to our goals.

Habits are often invisible, but without them, life would be so energy-draining. Imagine how inefficient it would be if you were constantly thinking about routine tasks. Think about your daily wake- up routine or your routine for getting to work or school, for ex-ample. You would soon be exhausted if you constantly had to be aware of each of your actions instead of running on autopilot for repetitive or routine tasks. Habits are invisible to us. We need to make a conscious effort to become aware of them, and even then, we might need someone to point them out to us. Habits make our lives easier. Even if they are bad habits, they free up time to do other things. That is why change is so hard. We need to re-create a pattern to make a change, and that takes a lot of energy.

Many people have habits that prevent them from being wealthy. When these habits are invisible, there is little we can do about them. We can't solve a problem if we are not aware of it. I analyzed what was preventing people from being comfortable or happy with their wealth. I call the results of my analysis the "unwealthy habits." If you are not satisfied with your wealth, it is worth taking a look at these unwealthy habits. It is as important to know what you are doing well as it is to know what you need to stop doing.

In this book, I present the cases of ten fictitious characters and examine their habits and their reasoning. Anna, Peter, Sophia, John, Carolyn, Mark, Joan, Tom, Lisa, and Paul are here to be observed and analyzed. By observing others, we learn much about ourselves. When you think, *"I am like So-and-so,* you are freer to observe than when you act. Don't get me wrong; taking action is fantastic, but *action limits refection.* Stop acting so that you can think about what you are doing.

I have compiled several cases because I know from my teaching experience that it is easier for us to solve other people's problems. We like to believe that we are perfect; as we say in my native country of Venezuela, "We carry our defects on a backpack," meaning that everybody sees them but us! And if someone points them out to us, we don't thank them but get defensive. Analyzing the cases of other people will make it easier for you to reflect freely without judging yourself. For some people, it might not be that relevant, but for others, talking about weaknesses, mistakes, and some times plain stupidity is hard—very hard.

You can make an analogy between the cases and your own unique situation and become aware of any particular habit that might be preventing you from reaching your goals. Observing how these habits are affecting others will help you assess your own behavior. Observing these cases will make it easier for you to find out if you are erecting barriers to achieving or maintaining your own financial well-being without realizing it.

Knowing about habits is not enough. You have to substitute wealthy habits for the unwealthy habits you discover. For each unwealthy habit, there is a specific set of thoughts and actions that creates a self-regulating system, setting you free from the habit. I call this system a "vaccine."

Before I continue, I would like to say a word of caution: wealth does not make you happy, but when you are wealthy you are happier. Why? Because you feel valued, important, respected, and appreciated. And, most important, because wealth gives you options, and you feel free. If you take care of your wealth, you stop worrying about it. You feel in control. However, you can feel valued and happy without feeling wealthy. Some of my best memories are from times when I was extremely poor.

We live in a world that confuses our essence with our successes. I prefer to think that we are our journey, not our destination. If there is no room for mistakes, there is no room for action. So this book is a refection that will help you take steps to stop doing what is holding you back, but it will not solve your problems. We take the journey one step at a time.

No matter how your life has been up to now, you can always look back and select your most memorable moments and your best learning experiences. Moments that made you feel you were in the perfect place at the perfect time. Moments that made you feel it was absolutely fantastic to be alive; experiences that altered your path, where you had to make a pivotal decision or you had to stop, reflect, and rethink; experiences that felt like life was teaching you a lesson, not asking you for questions but giving you the opportunity to learn. This process of 'selective' history means taking your best moments to leverage on, and the worst to learn and become a better person. Having a way to select your history prepares you to continue your journey.

You cannot change your past, but you can choose to look back selectively and see what empowers you and what drains your energy. In both cases, it is the same past, but it is not the same present. By picking your best moments and choosing to reflect upon your mistakes in order to learn, you shape your future.

I started by reflecting on what had made a difference in my own journey. I moved from working and saving, to losing all my funds because of a banking crisis and being almost broke, to getting a job, to managing an investment fund, to retiring before I was forty-five years old. Yet my own experience was not enough. As a former scientist and engineer, I know that we need more data than what comes from just one sample. Thus, I analyzed what others were telling me. I researched. I became curious. I asked, and then I organized the ideas into categories and refined them until I had summarized the most common barriers into the ten unwealthy habits people unknowingly build that interfere with their views of their wealth.

Numbers, however, don't do us justice. You are not invisible, lost as a nameless number on a statistics paper; you are a person—unique, valuable, and special. Some of these habits will not apply to you, or you might discover slight variations. Other habits will be reassuring and comforting to you, and you might not want to think about changing them. I hope that an awareness of these habits will benefit your life, but it is up to you to decide if it will.

To start, read the list of habits on the list of content and choose the one or ones that resonate with you. Pick a character and follow that person's story. What would you tell that person? How would you help him or her overcome that habit? Those are the lessons you might be dealing with and your suggestions will be the suggestions you do need to hear.

Remember, it is necessary both to have wealthy habits and to overcome unwealthy habits. In this book, the discussion is only about unwealthy habits. There is a lot of information and support for getting you on the right financial track. Do your part and enjoy the ride. In the end, everything will be fine. If it is not fine, it's not the end.

Alicia Castillo Holley
www.thetenunwealthyhabits.com

Habit #1:
Feeling
Sorry
for
Yourself

Feeling Sorry for Yourself

Anna feels sorry for herself because she is a woman; men have better options.

Peter feels sorry for himself because he is black; whites don't have to face racism.

Sophia feels sorry for herself because she is fat; skinny people get better jobs.

John feels sorry for himself because he is short; taller people have a greater appeal and are more impressive.

Carolyn feels sorry for herself because she is too skinny; other people look healthier.

Mark feels sorry for himself because he is single; married people have someone who loves them.

Joan feels sorry for herself because she is married; single people have more fun.

Tom feels sorry for himself because he is divorced; married people don't pay child support.

Lisa feels sorry for herself because she is young; older people get more respect.

Paul feels sorry for himself because he is old; younger people have more energy.

Unwealthy people think that life is unfair. Injustice plays a big role in their lives; they are frustrated by things over which they have no control. They don't realize that thinking that life is unfair prevents them from making good decisions.

Feeling Sorry for Yourself

IF YOU FEEL SORRY FOR YOURSELF, how do you expect others to feel about you?

Unwealthy people focus on what is wrong with their lives…
> and focus on it…
> and focus on it…

In the process, they spread negativity. Feeling sorry for oneself is the most common of the invisible unwealthy habits. We all have circumstances outside of our control that limit our capacity to do things freely. Life is evenly unfair.

Although we do not control everything, nobody controls our attitude but us. Life is not fair or just; it is just life.

Let's look at Anna's case. Her feelings of self-pity permeate the way she connects to the world and spread the feeling of helplessness. She is prone to making statements that validate her self-pity and end with something like, "because I am a woman." Her female listeners have only two options: to share in her misery of being a woman or to feel or think differently and try to take a more positive approach.

If they share her feelings, they feed into her habit of feeling sorry for herself, and the result is a shared feeling of disappointment, which is not to be confused with compassion. If they choose the more positive option, they can't express empathy,.

However her listeners react, there is a single true statement that nobody can change: Anna is a woman. Unless there are more serious issues, it is easier and more practical for Anna to change her feelings about being a woman than for her to undergo a sex change.

Feeling sorry for oneself is one of the most useless of feelings. Life is what it is. It does have its hardships, but self-pity does not help anybody. In my book *Falling in Love with Your Life*, I explain how to move from being a victim to being a hero. Our attitudes create different results even if the circumstances don't change. We are not our circumstances; we are our attitudes. Success, like happiness, is inside of us trying to get out—not outside trying to get in.

One young woman asked me at a conference if I ever felt things were harder for me because I was a woman. My response was as direct as I could make it. "Yes," I replied, "they were. I was born and raised in a developing country; I have a small body; I look naively young; and I could list many other factors. Yet, who wants a boring life? I could have been disabled or lived in a worse country. My circumstances don't make me; I am more than that." The trick is not to fall into feeling sorry for ourselves. It does not change a thing!"

Discrimination and rejection live as much in ourselves as in others. I refuse to have pity on myself or any other human being, simply because pity does not help anyone overcome difficulties.

Feeling sorry for yourself is like an anchor; it prevents you from living fully and enjoying your life. It does nothing to provide joy, happiness, fun, and support to others; and it contributes nothing to your requests for help, love, and commitment.

Feeling sorry for yourself is a great way to sell your life short, to occupy your time with identifying what you are missing in life and justify why you can't do what you want. You could use that same energy and time to find ways to overcome barriers, educate others, break paradigms, and change the world.

Feeling sorry for yourself diminishes the value you expect, create, and demand from others. You cannot be wealthy if you are feeling sorry for yourself. And believe me, if you continue to feel sorry for yourself, you will find plenty of reasons to convince yourself of your own bad luck.

So, what can you do? Saying, "I am not going to feel sorry for myself," does not work, nor can you pretend to believe that your problems do not exist. We know, we all know, that there are some external barriers that keep us from getting where we want to be. Ignoring them doesn't work, but there is one thing that does: diminishing the importance of those barriers.

The vaccine against feelings of self-pity is gratitude. Focusing on what is going well in your life creates a cycle of pride and healthy selfishness. It sets you up on a more powerful platform of giving your best and expecting the best. It builds your confidence.

When you focus on what is fantastic about your life, you feel blessed, content, unique, and valuable, and it shows. You work on your strengths, on your passions, on your best you. You focus on making the best of your life, including taking responsibility for your resources. Your life as it is does not change, but your attitude does. With that change, you can change your life. You create a virtuous cycle: When you feel fortunate, you make better choices. When you make better choices, you create better moments, develop healthier conversations, and have no time for self-pity.

Habit #2:

Being

Greedy

Being Greedy

Anna does not pay full price for her shoes; she buys them on sale.

Peter looks for bargains at garage sales; he does not buy anything new.

Sophia hires part-time workers so she doesn't have to pay benefits.

John uses his frequent-flier miles to pay for vacation flights, choosing the best deals.

Carolyn also uses her reward miles for all her electronic products at home, even if they don't match.

Mark's employer paid for his MBA, but not at the university of his choice.

Joan demands upgrades from all her suppliers; she knows they won't want to lose a client.

Tom never pays overtime; he wants hardworking employees.

Lisa buys her clothes from online sales, even though she can't try them on.

Paul feels his children should work for their allowance and clothing; he didn't get help, either.

Unwealthy people focus on maximizing what they get for their money in- stead of choosing freely. They love "a great value" and seek opportunities to make the most of whatever resources they have, without considering any other variable. They don't realize that focusing on "getting a good deal" leaves them with a low sense of worth and prevents them from creating opportunities to increase their revenue.

Being Greedy

IF YOU ARE TOO WORRIED ABOUT SPENDING YOUR MONEY and feel you are going to run out of resources, you can be missing opportunities to enjoy what you truly want, or you could be failing to use the time to find ways to increase your wealth.

You cannot be wealthy unless you distribute part of your wealth. It is refreshing to feel that you can afford something you want, and, subconsciously or not, it feeds your sense of contribution by allowing you to value others' work and participate in their well-being. Your struggle to determine the value of products and services feeds your expectation that people do not recognize your real value.

Let's explore Peter's case. He adores a garage sale and loves finding a great bargain, especially if it is something new for almost nothing. Furthermore, Peter rarely buys anything new at all; he prefers to buy "pre-loved" products. He and his family spend most weekends browsing for good deals. He brags about his smart shopping habit and how he hasn't bought anything at "full price" for five years. However, some of the products he purchased are stored somewhere because they don't fit with or match what he already has. Furthermore, he has also missed out on the feeling of deciding what he wants and the feeling that he can afford a treat. Because his focus is on how much he is saving, he exchanges his freedom to buy what he really wants for the alternative of buying what someone else once wanted and is now discarding. He uses his free time to find bargains for things that he does not need or want.

People who are constantly talking about how to make the most of their money can make others around them feel lazy, wasteful, or insecure. Not only do they intimate that they are smarter because they beat the system, they can also send a subconscious message about making someone else lose out and can fail to acknowledge the true value of the time and efforts of others.

We all love a great deal, but making the most of every single purchase is time-consuming and unwealthy. If you are getting a great deal, chances are that someone else is subsidizing your gain or taking a loss. Ultimately, wealth is destroyed.

Unwealthy people focus on their expenses as if their wealth were fixed. They fail to see their wealth as a flow that balances what comes in (income, value, pleasure) and what goes out (expenses, time). Their habit becomes unwealthy when they fail to realize the true value of their expenditures.

When I asked Peter to tear a one-dollar bill, he couldn't do it. Yet he was willing to spend countless hours and hundreds of dollars per month on products and services that were useless to him and his family because they were "good deals."

Focusing on making the absolute most of every transaction is tiring. Greedy people only enjoy what they have if they make the most of it or brag about how they have outsmarted others—other clients or other suppliers. When people act greedy, they feel an imbalance in what comes in and what goes out. They squeeze those who provide goods and services that make life easier, better, more pleasurable, and more efficient. Pursuing a great value for the money at the expense of others has a negative effect on society

as a whole. Suppliers of greedy people don't feel valued, can't afford reason- able expenses, and tend to be greedy themselves. To make matters worse, greedy people expect others to be greedy too, and they themselves don't feel valued or appreciated.

The vaccine against feeling greedy is to choose freely. Focus on what you enjoy, respect your own ability to provide for yourself, and balance your wealth as a flow of resources (time, value, money). This is a healthier way to manage your finances. Choosing what you want freely, regardless of whether or not it is a great deal, is the best way to break free of greed. This was a difficult habit for me to break. I love great deals, but now price is only one component of my purchasing decisions, not the most important one— and definitely not the only one.

You can break free of being greedy when you rank the benefits of a service or product over and above the price you pay for it. For example, when we support local businesses, even if the prices are higher, we feel that we contribute to our community by supporting local jobs. Crime and depression are lower in supportive communities. A client once asked me if I would be willing to pay an over- seas programmer if the fee was cheaper. I answered that I would consider my other costs in the equation, such as my time and well-being and the time it would take for transfers of information and funding. I do hire people around the world, as my businesses are global, but I take into consideration other factors besides the price. We need to use common sense. I am not in favor of being over- indulgent (another unwealthy habit), but focusing our purchasing decisions solely on great deals is detrimental to our communities, our pockets, and our hearts.

Be free in your choice and responsible about what you want. If you can't afford something, save or increase your revenue until you can. Become aware of how you, too, contribute to the wheel of the wealth of others by making good choices. When you believe in fair value, it shows. You give and take based on your expectations, and you can feel proud to be able to afford what you want and to give others the opportunity to be valuable to you. You also have more free time to enjoy life and explore ways to increase your income. Wealthy people feel happy about their roles in the wealth of others and have a higher perception of their value to the world. They also put a high value on their time.

Habit #3:

Hating

What

You

Do

Hating What You Do

Anna hates doing dishes, but she doesn't consider any other options.

Peter hates walking his dog, but he has to do so every day.

Sophia hates dancing, but she can't throw away the time and money she has already spent studying dance.

John hates fast food, but it is the only way to eat at lunchtime.

Carolyn hates driving, but she is not going to take public transportation or consider carpooling.

Mark hates his job, but he needs to pay the mortgage.

Joan hates archiving, but that is all she can do without a college degree.

Tom hates selling, but it is the only way to get clients for his business.

Lisa hates consulting, but it is the best-paying job she can get.

Paul hates working in the winter, but he can't afford to move out of Boston.

Unwealthy people think that life is hard and that they have no alterna- tives to doing what they dislike. They compromise. They feel that there is a realistic expectation that they have to do some things even if they don't want to. They don't look for alternatives because they can't even imagine them.

Hating What You Do

IF YOU ALLOW YOURSELF TO BE TRAPPED into doing something you hate for long enough, you will become really bad at it. The most successful people have learned to treasure their time and spend most of it on what they enjoy most, what they are most passionate about, and what they thrive at, and they stick to that. The things they don't like doing, they delegate to others.

When you do things you hate, you become resentful, and it shows, resulting in rejection from others. When you spend time doing what you love, you gain a sense of fulfillment that is almost magical. By choosing to spend time on what you are passionate about, you can learn, explore, and thrive. Wealthy people have high expectations for their time. They use it wisely, as they know it is the *only* limiting asset.

Nowadays, we have access to so much information that we for- get to be ourselves, and we try to be more like everybody else. No wonder we believe that if we don't like doing something, nobody else with a sound mind would like doing it either.

For example, I used to think that nobody could like doing dishes. Washing dishes was a source of frustration for me for many years—until I met people who were not so hung up about it. Some even liked washing dishes, especially if someone else cooked, because they hated cooking! If you don't like doing a specific task, find away to let somebody else do it. That is the beauty of diversity. Even if you can't pay for someone else's work, explore an exchange.

Getting stuck in doing things we strongly dislike is damaging. We can't excel, and nobody appreciates our work. We get into a vicious cycle. How do you feel when you know you hate what you are doing? How do you feel when you know that another person hates what he or she is doing? This is an unwealthy habit, because the value of what you do is highly related to your sense of excellence and fun. Unwealthy people focus on how much money they are making or on how they are maximizing their natural abilities to make more money. It is an invisible trap. Unwealthy people's focus is on the money, either on making it or on not spending it. This unwealthy habit—hating what you do—prevents you from earning a living by doing what you are passionate about. The previous unwealthy habit—being greedy—keeps you from spending your money on whatever you are passionate about. In both cases, money is running the show, and that is unwealthy.

When you accept things you detest into your life, you become mediocre at those things; you feel less worthy, and you can't find the passion to excel. Therefore, you miss the opportunity to give life your best shot, and what is worse, you give out a certain message about yourself: I don't care about the use of my time; I can't do things well; and I am available to be abused.

There is a clear distinction between doing what you are passionate about and further developing your natural skills. Some people excel at activities they end up hating. Take Sophia's case. As a child, she performed in a number of school plays. She loved ballet and worked relentlessly to become a ballerina, only to discover that she did not like the sweating, the endless practices, and the late nights. She was a good dancer, yet she began to hate dancing. Her natural skills diminished with time, as she did not enjoy her career. Fortunately for Sophia, she decided to shift careers. She loved the stage but didn't like acting or singing. She forced herself to make a change and became a model, although not a good one, and then a manager for a ballet company. Later in life, she became an interior decorator. She loves the sense of harmony and beauty interior decorating gives her, and she now thrives in her work. She loves her new life, and it shows in the way she talks to her clients and devotes herself to finding new choices for them. Sophia spent three decades of her life trying to make a living by leveraging her natural skills and the time and money she had spent on her training, instead of fulfilling her passion.

She thought she wouldn't be able to make a decent living as an interior decorator. She loved doing it so much that she didn't think anyone would actually pay her. Other clients of mine have also had unusual forms of expertise. One of my clients went from accounting to biking. I went from science to finance to writing. The trick is to shift your thinking from, *How can I make money?* to *What do I enjoy doing most?*

The vaccine against doing things you hate is demanding the best from your time. Shift your mind-set. Don't aim to do what you are best at; do what you enjoy most. You can do that by focusing on what you are passionate about and by delegating or outsourcing those tasks you don't like doing. In doing so, you also get rid of the arrogant attitude that you are irreplaceable. Guess what. You are not. Someone will always be better, more efficient, more creative, more productive, and more experienced at any single thing you do. If you love what you do, you will reach out to those experts and learn from them instead of resent them.

Wealthy people are more focused and selective about how they spend their time. Doing what you are passionate about brings out the best in you, almost despite your natural abilities. Other people might point out that you have to do what you are best at. Reconsider their suggestions based on what you want to do, as these other people are judging your skills using different and unique sets of references. People who do not have your skills will value them and often with the best of intentions will comment on what you should do. For example, I admire people who can draw, because I can't and it does not interest me enough to learn. I tend to think that anybody with a capacity to draw would want to become an illustrator. However, I no longer think or say, "You are so good at this; you should do it for a living," as I used to.

What you are best at does not necessarily bring out the best in you, unless of course what you are best at is also what you are most passionate about. By liberating yourself from the burden of doing things you hate, you can focus and start to excel at what you enjoy most and begin to explore what helps you thrive. Feeling trapped by the thinking, *I have to do things I hate*, is a perfect way of earning disrespect from ourselves and others. The only thing we have to do is die; everything else we do because we choose to.

If you stop doing what you hate doing, your life will be better, and chances are that another person will be passionate about what you dislike. Even if that does not happen, you owe it to yourself to be accountable and responsible for your own well-being. To you, you are first. That is what I call "healthy selfishness." If you feel responsible for a specific task that you don't like doing, delegate or outsource it and supervise, but don't spend your most valuable asset, your time, doing things that don't thrill you.

Explore ways to stop doing what you dislike. Demanding the most of your time is not an easy exercise. Many books and experts talk about the importance of having fun. Basically, when you have high expectations of your time, you shift to doing tasks that bring positive energy into your life. The world does not deteriorate if we don't do what we don't like doing. Somehow, there will be a new balance. The world won't change drastically, but your life will.

If you don't know what you are passionate about, chances are that you have too much "noise" from external opinions. Remember that others will see your skills based on their own weaknesses. People's capacity to make the transition from what they are best at to what they love doing varies. Some people are successful by many measurements, but they don't love what they do. It is never too late to do what you are passionate about.

When you are passionate about something, you experience a state of optimal experience, as defined by Mihaly Csikszentmihalyi in his book, *Flow: The Psychology of Optimal Experiences*. You are experiencing "the flow" when you feel that time is not passing; you en- joy what you are doing so much that you feel energized, inspired, and willing to learn, grow, make mistakes, take criticism, and be curious.

When you demand the best of your time, you become more valuable, attractive, and enjoyable. Your conversations improve, and so do your decisions and outcomes.

Habit #4: Using Money to Measure Happiness

Using Money to Measure Happiness

Anna can't wait to have more money so she can move to a bigger house.

Peter can't wait to have more money so he can get tailor-made clothing.

Sophia can't wait to have more money so she can go out more.

John can't wait to have more money so he can travel overseas.

Carolyn can't wait to have more money so she can get her children what she didn't have.

Mark can't wait to have more money so he can become more attractive to women.

Joan can't wait to have more money so she doesn't have to be dependent on her husband.

Tom can't wait to have more money so he can become an artist.

Lisa can't wait to have more money so she can support a local charity.

Paul can't wait to have more money so he can retire and stop working.

Unwealthy people think money drives happiness. They think the more money a person has, the happier he or she is, and vice versa. For them, however, happiness is perpetually waiting to happen, because they think about their wealthier future and they feel they need more, regardless of how much they already have right now.

Using Money to Measure Happiness

THINKING THAT HAPPINESS IS RELATED TO MONEY is an old paradigm. Wanting more money is fine, but not when that desire prevents you from enjoying the present. Money gives you choices to a certain extent, but it does not give you happiness. Stefan frames it very well in his book, *The Science of Happiness*, claims that ouur sense of joy is not related to our choices; it is related to our emotions. The choices of a peasant in rural China are very different from the choices of a wealthy model in New York, yet their feelings of happiness and accomplishment are similar.

Very few people are comfortable with the concept of money or wealth. Some people pursue money as their only means to happiness, while others perceive being wealthy as a barrier to happiness.

We all know stories of the poor family in which there was so much love that they did not need money and of the rich family whose lives were horrible because they had so much envy and drama. These stories are told by people who need to justify why they are not wealthy. It is fine to want more money and to have a purpose for that money. I have been both poor and rich. I prefer to be rich, but I am a happy person regardless.

Wealthy people make a distinction between wealth and happiness.

They know that money does not give happiness. Our joy and pleasure come from feelings associated with what we do —feelings such as love, security, power, and generosity—not what we have or from money itself.

Unwealthy people think consciously or unconsciously that money buys happiness. They relate the amount of money or the possessions they have to their happiness, only to realize that they are no happier after they get what they want. If you want more money so that you can enjoy your life, it is time for you to stop and think about ways in which you can enjoy your life right now.

Money is an illusion; we don't like money so much as we like what we can do with it. Tracking down the benefits of having money and clarifying them can help you understand what you really want. Once you understand and experience that money does not make you happy, you are able to focus on what you love; as a result, you are able to work better and have more joy in your life and more free time to think creatively about making money in a way that fills your wallet but also fulfills your other intellectual, emotional, and spiritual needs.

Let's look at John's case. John has been saving for three years to travel around the world. As a high achiever, he plans to spend four months visiting exotic places and wants to be reassured that he will be able to afford his trip and support himself while he looks for a new job upon returning home. He has read several books, consulted Web sites, and even picked his top twenty-three cities. When I asked John what he liked best within a fifty-mile radius of his home, he could not answer. He had not visited the local Vietnamese church, the Singaporean restaurant, the French creperie, or the Ethiopian shop. Furthermore, he could not name one place in his hometown that could be called a tourist attraction. Peter was surprised to learn about less-expensive options for traveling around the world; he had also not considered that he could work for room and board while traveling or that he could be a volunteer or even an expatriate employee. As a matter of fact, he learned that working overseas would be great for his résumé.

The single most important change in John's attitude came when he realized that he wanted to feel a sense of adventure and to explore the unknown and that he could experience those things within only a few miles of where he lived and worked. He changed his habit of waiting to have money to do what he wanted, and he started enjoying the diversity within his own community. He took some language courses, participated in online discussions, took a short trip to volunteer as an English teacher in a neighboring country, and started enjoying his worldwide trip before it happened.

The vaccine against using money to measure wealth is to find inner joy in the present. Wealthy people put themselves first; they enjoy their lives—and spend responsibly. Money is a part of the equation, but it is not the entire equation. While money does broaden their choices, wealthy people realize it does not give them happiness. They focus on their feelings.

For example, I've always spent both time and money on something that gives me great pleasure: eating. When I could afford it, I took my children and parents to a nice restaurant once a month; it was a treat for all of us. When I was a student working on my MBA and had very little money, all we could afford was a trip to a local dough-nut shop where my children got to share a single doughnut. We paid a lot less for those doughnuts than we did for those dinners we ate at nice restaurants when I was working full-time months before. We felt wealthy anyway, because we celebrated going out for a treat and sharing food in a special way. We focused on our feelings.

When you practice enjoying the present moment, you get out of the rat race. The way you view the world changes, and the world views you differently as well.

You don't need money to be happy. Furthermore, you don't need money to do those things you want to do. Most people share the belief that we need money to do things. We make sensible plans based on what is accepted by the majority. Usually, we see how others have achieved their goals and try to emulate them. If you think you need a degree, a car, a sixty-hour workweek, a great body, or whatever else to be successful, you will think and act accordingly. You will even find ways to validate your perceptions by talking to others and getting their agreement and reassurance. The challenge is to expand your boundaries and think about how you can achieve the results you want in your own unique ways. Some people even choose not to work for money at all, and somehow, it works.

The way we manage our lives resides in our brains. We set our goals first, and then we reach them. The point is to work on our goals; once we set them and begin to focus on how to get there, we can make it. If you think you need money to make you happy, start thinking about what it is you want to do with that money once you get it. What do you want to do with the money you are waiting for? Is there any substitute? What can you do if you don't have the money you need now? Change your thinking from, I *need* to, so it becomes I *want* to. Such a change will have a liberating effect on the way you view wealth, and you will feel in control.

When you shift from "have to" to "want to," your life improves dramatically. No, you don't *need* to pay the mortgage or the car payment or the credit card bill; you *choose* to, because it gives you a sense of fulfillment, value, importance, responsibility, self-esteem, curiosity, integrity, and contribution.

When you realize that happiness is inside of you and that money is an illusion, you actually attract more money. You realize that you are already wealthy.

Having more or less money doesn't have anything to do with feeling more or less happy, unless we make that association ourselves.

Habit #5:
Overspending

Overspending

Anna overspends on food; she goes to great restaurants even if she can't pay rent.

Peter overspent on his car; it was a great deal, and he had always wanted to have that model.

Sophia overspent on her house; she needed more space and a better location.

John overspends on clothing; he must look smart and successful.

Carolyn overspent on her education; she thought she needed two master's degrees to secure a good job.

Mark overspends on dinners and dates; it is the only way to impress ladies.

Joan overspends on everything; she doesn't have anything else to do during the day.

Tom overspends on his children; he needs to make sure they know he loves them.

Lisa overspends on traveling; she will get out of debt later.

Paul overspends on sports; he has to do it now before he is too old to enjoy it.

Unwealthy people think that it is normal to be stressed about paying for things that they cannot afford. Because they are overwhelmed with their spending habits, they allow money to take happiness away from their lives. Money does not make you happy, but overspending can take hap- piness away from you.

Overspending

UNDERSTANDING THE CONCEPT OF OVERSPENDING is simple: you spend more than you earn. Overspending is like trying to hold water with a strainer; the money flows out and cannot be contained. People who overspend have several pressure points being hit at the same time:

~ they need to balance money and time very carefully;

~ they are scared about not paying some things on time;

~ their costs are higher because of short-term high interest;
~ they feel trapped into doing things they dislike because of the need to pay for things they've purchased;

~ they sell themselves short because of debt;

~ they don't feel "smart" about the way they spend money, and as a consequence, they have low self-esteem.

People overspend because they don't see a way out. They have so much debt that they feel there is no way to get back on track. They don't trust themselves.

Unwealthy people fail to evaluate the overall impact of their over-spending in their lives. They live to the limits of their spending or even above it. They have not experienced living in a wealthy manner, meaning having more income than expenses. They feel their lives are filled with needs that are never satisfied. Wealth people don't need to limit their spending, because they know that they can manage it.

When people overspend, they put money first and their lives second, and they get into a trap of unhappiness. That creates an unnecessary cycle of worries. Worrying about money eats your happiness away. If you don't take care of your wealth, your wealth will preoccupy you and prevent you from enjoying life. Suze Orman mentioned once that many overspenders make purchases to impress people they don't even know! We all want to be recognized as being successful, yet our peace of mind needs to come first. Authenticity is a much more powerful way of gaining respect and admiration than overspending. If you worry about what others think about your wealth and you struggle to meet their expectations, you are not being kind to yourself.

There are many programs that can help you get out of debt, manage your finances, and cut your spending. Sometimes there is an emergency that disrupts your planned—even well-planned— strategy. I saved for five years to study for an MBA only to lose my savings to a banking crisis. I could have chosen to feel sorry or angry for the rest of my life or get over it. I realized, however, that the best thing I could do was learn from the experience.

Wealth is a flow; it relates what comes in to what goes out. If you build a dam and the amount of water that goes over the dam is larger than the amount that comes into the pool behind it, your supply will eventually empty. You can take some bets by diverting rivers, but you need to be willing to take the consequences of failure.

Let's look at Carolyn's case, a case I particularly like. As a firm believer in education, I never thought anybody could overspend on it. Carolyn was determined to get the best education possible. She worked part-time while she was in college and decided to continue on to a second master's degree after finishing her first one. Her options with financial aid were limited because she had neither great grades nor experience. While she was working toward her degree, she continued to work part-time, which limited her studying time. Despite being careful with her expenses, she accumulated a considerable amount of debt, including undergraduate and graduate tuition, plus some of her living expenses. What Carolyn failed to consider was the cost of debt. After seven years of studies, she was overworked, stressed, tired, and broke. She was on the verge of a nervous breakdown, spending her few free moments blaming herself.

Let me take a break to explain something about debt. When you think about debt, you need to think about principal (the total amount borrowed, yes, including fees) plus interest and fees related to the interest (the cost of capital). It is very expensive to be poor. Debt is expensive. While there are some circumstances in which it makes sense to overspend, such as if you are making a sensitive investment, analyze the real cost of any loan and you will be amazed at what you will end up paying.

From a lender's perspective, ideal loans pay interest forever. Unwealthy people try to reduce payments by not including principal, so the interest continues to roll. Wealthy people reduce payments by paying more principal and get rid of the payment altogether. Because Carolyn had not been able to pay off any part of the principal, her original debt increased by twenty-five percent while she worked on her two-year master's program. Her focus was on spending on education, not on evaluating the use of that investment and profiting from the investment she had made on her education. When you are overspending, you must plan carefully so you can get rid of the payment altogether by paying off the principal. Such a plan will increase your payments in the short term, but it will get you out of debt.

I want to explain how being poor and getting into debt is so expensive with real numbers, and I will use my numbers to make this point. I decided to go to the United States despite the fact that I had lost five years of savings due to a banking crisis. With only $1,700, I moved from Venezuela to Boston. I had a scholarship and a loan, yet I was not able to lower my living expenses to match my income. The only option for survival was to spend more than I earned, to overspend. It took me two years to accumulate my educational debt, but it took me eight years and careful planning to pay off my debt at the annual interest rates of eighteen percent on fourteen cred- it cards and of seventy-eight percent on a government loan from my home country. The government loan at seventy-eight percent had only made sense because I assumed our currency would be devalued, which turned out to be what happened. However, the annual cost of my debt was almost as much as the amount I had originally borrowed. Like Carolyn, I had overspent on education. Unlike hers, my interest rates were ridiculously high, but the rapid increase in my earnings after I acquired my degree and the devaluation of bolívares, my country's currency, made up for that cost. Because I earned money in United States dollars instead of my in country's currency and because of the devaluation, over the course of ten years my payments went from $18,000 per year to only $400 per year. I had made a good yet risky decision, and it put a great deal of pressure on my need to work. As a result, I overworked for years. We took many trips to doughnut and ice cream shops as treats until I was comfortable with my debts.

The vaccine against overspending is planning. Fix your expenses. Wealthy people put aside a percentage of their income for enjoyment, and they spend that piece fully on whatever gives them pleasure, but they also save some of their income to invest. The formula that has worked for me is 10-10-10-70. I spend ten percent on indulgence, ten percent on savings, ten percent on donations, and I live with the remaining seventy percent or less. When I did not have much money, I used my time as a resource.

Even as my priorities and needs have changed, I still take time and money to enjoy myself, to invest, and to donate. I also like having both active and passive income. I like working and actively earning an income as well as having investments that require little of my time to generate a return.

Comprehending the difference between passive income and active income is important, so this concept is worth more discussion. Active income is, in fact, directly related to the use of your time, whereas passive income is not. Many people will define passive income as what you can earn without using your time. That is false; you will always need to spend some time revisiting your finances and making changes that suit your present situation.

When people talk about passive income, they have to consider their time spent on things such as development, follow-up, sales, analysis, and so forth. The claim that you can make money without effort does not make sense to me. Your financial responsibility is personal and nontransferable. If someone is telling you that you don't need to work to gain passive income, you are being lied to.

Wealthy people don't forego being accountable for their results. For example, I don't have the passion to invest in shares of public companies. I prefer to invest in start-ups where I can support, influence, and make strategic decisions. Investing in others' decisions about how to run a business is not my cup of tea. Because I don't like investing in public companies, I don't fall into the trap of doing things I am not passionate about. Yet there are many interesting opportunities in that market. So, I use a fantastic group that manages that aspect of my investing for me. They are passionate about investing in public companies, and my conversations with members of that group are great fun. Twice a year, together, we discuss my strategy, and they implement it. I listen to their suggestions, and they listen to my comments. They are the experts, but it is my money. If they mess up, they might lose a client, but I lose my money. So I need to be comfortable with what they are doing. It is passive income, because I can't relate the amount of time I spend on it to the results. The same thing applies to writing books. The income I generate from writing is not related to my time spent writing or promoting books.

Carolyn's breakthrough came from a simple shift. Instead of using her limited free time on understanding how the problem came into existence, she began to explore solutions.

Every minute spent worrying about a problem is a minute wasted. Instead, explore solutions. In Carolyn's case, she realized that time spent using her education to find higher-paying jobs was the key to earning more income. Carolyn had to think differently in two more ways: she had to believe in her own capacity to overcome her challenges, and she had to design and implement a plan. She had to work less at low-paying jobs and focus on securing higher-paying jobs in order to repay her debt. She had to trust herself to follow through and to use any failure as a learning opportunity to test herself. The thought of breaking out of debt and crafting a smart financial strategy to live off her investments was a powerful motivator to keep her on track.

Wealthy people prefer to feel smart about the way they handle their resources and feel good about their spending choices, because how they feel about their resources is more important than whatever gratification they get from their purchases. Eventually, savings become large enough to invest; the investments generate income that accumulates, and slowly but steadily, their passive income becomes larger and larger.

Wealthy people live off their investments. They work for pleasure, not for money. Keep this in mind to help you achieve your financial goals. You can do it if you work at it, even if you make mistakes, including bankruptcy. To start or to continue on your plan, the rule is simple: what comes in has to be greater than what goes out. Wealthy people are smart about handling that difference.

To manage your spending, create your ideal spending pattern and compromise with yourself. Include the full cost of debt; that is, the cost of interest plus fees, plus the cost of your time spent handling debt. The way you handle your debt has to be as simple, large, or complex as your debt is. In some cases, you might choose to sell your house or car, to downsize, to move to a less expensive city, or to take even more drastic actions. The best part is that it is never too late to start. We'll talk more about this in the discussion about the next habit.

Many people fail to keep their commitments because they have other unwealthy habits and because they forget to reward themselves. Make sure to include a reward, even if it is a walk, a pat on the back, or a one-dollar doughnut. Be comfortable with your spending. When in doubt, remember that money does not give you happiness, but it can take it away from you.

Habit #6: Preferring Instant Gratification

Preferring Instant Gratification

Anna eats at expensive restaurants; you don't know how long you'll live.

Peter wanted his car so much, he couldn't say no to buying it.

Sophia thought she deserved a bigger house; it made her feel successful.

John dresses in the latest trends in business suits; it's a way to impress.

Carolyn got right into her master's degree program because everyone told her she needed it.

Mark wants to show he is wealthy so he can develop relationships with winners.

Joan can't resist online shopping; that way she buys the latest fashion before anyone else.

Tom feels his children are too demanding, but he can't let them down.

Lisa travels in luxury; she wants to enjoy her life now before she gets too old.

Paul has a garage full of sports gadgets; even if he uses them only once, he wants the "pro" look.

Unwealthy people use their present to sabotage their future. They don't take care of their resources in a way that makes their wealth increase with time. They misconstrue the philosophy of "living in the present" and forget that the future is built today, not yesterday and not tomorrow. They feel that not having something now implies not having it in the future.

Preferring Instant Gratification

WHEN YOU GET INTO THE TRAP of thinking that the future is now, you fail to plan for your future. It is a simple fact that the future is ahead, the past is behind, and the present is now. The present moment is the only one we have any power to change.

Unwealthy people don't understand that the future is affected by the past. They look back and feel anxious. Their past has not been used to build a foundation of wealth. They never planned, or they planned poorly, or they were unlucky. In the worst cases, they look back at their lives and simply are not capable of reflecting upon how their past choices affected their present. Their past is neither a building block nor a learning experience. Because they have never planned for the future, they don't think they can start now.

In reality, even if you plan for the future, things can go wrong. I have lived through some unforeseen circumstances that were completely out of my control. Still, I personally don't believe in luck, either good or bad. Anyway, luck is out of my control, so why even worry about it? I prefer to think and feel that I control my destiny. Wealthy people know that luck follows good decisions and preparedness. They do their best to get the best outcomes.

Unwealthy people are more concerned about doing it all now without considering the implications for the long run. They fail to reflect upon the impact of important financial decisions they make today. They fail to think that every action generates a reaction. If today's actions sabotage tomorrow, change today. It is the only way to change tomorrow. Nobody can change the past, but anybody can choose how to use the past to make a better future.

Unwealthy people have difficulty visualizing or relating their current choices to their future, just as they have difficulty relating past choices to their present. In many instances, it is simply a case of not thinking about it. Just that!

Let's look at Mark's case. He wants to show he is wealthy so he can develop relationships with successful people. His philosophy is: "You fake it and fake it and fake it until you make it." He knows that he is at his best right now and is not willing to compromise luxury for peace of mind. Mark has the look, the car, the golf club, the gym—you name it. He loves the feeling of luxury and of being surrounded by people who are generous in their spending. Mark has made some good decisions and got a great deal on his MBA. He needs to prove that he can afford his lifestyle, despite the fact that doing so limits his capacity to save. Mark is a smart person and likes to feel comfortable about his choices. Although his debt is manageable, he is not able to save; therefore, he cannot invest or take risks freely. He can't see himself as wealthy in the future. Recently, he participated in a pool investment and spent hours worrying miserably about how it would turn out. He just wasn't comfortable with the risk he had taken with his hard-earned money. He faked an emergency and pulled out. His friends and acquaintances can't relate to his worries because they have more abundance. He feels left out and inadequate. He is faking it, but he is not making it. Constant worry hangs like a cloud from which rain never pours down.

The vaccine against instant gratification is planning. The easiest way to achieve a goal is to plan. Without goals, planning is impossible.

Without a plan, goals become unattainable. When we create a habit of reflecting upon our actions and relating our decisions to our outcomes, we get better results. In my work with businesses, I find that most businesses fail not because they failed to plan but because they forgot to evaluate whether the actions they were taking led them to the goals they wanted. Most people don't have a plan that they can relate to. They don't have objective goals that are measurable; therefore, they can't evaluate how their past, present, and future decisions are related. Luck, not their decisions, is running their lives.

Let's look at how time relationships work. Wealthy people are comfortable with taking actions in the present to build their wealth for the future using their learning from the past. They know that man- aging the flow of their wealth in the present is critical to their well- being, peace of mind, and enjoyment in the future. They change their "have to" statements into "want to" statements.

Wealthy people have a safety cushion and money to invest in opportunities because they plan. Their money flow is balanced between what goes in and what goes out in a way that there is a build-up (savings) that creates two levels of peace of mind. First, a safety cushion covers any unexpected expenses, and second, they have the capacity to win and lose by investing. Their savings are there- fore tied both to a cushion and to future investments. That is the trick! Wealthy people can actually enjoy delaying gratification be- cause they know that they will be able to afford things later by using the results of their investments (passive income) and not their direct income (active income). They plan in order to "have to" do less and "want to" do more.

Wealthy people first save to build a safety cushion in case of emer- gencies. After they build this untouchable safety cushion, they can start an investment program using other savings. Their future expenses can be covered by the income from their investments and not by their active income. They can afford to take some risks be- cause they have a safety cushion to fall back on.

Let's explore further how wealthy people manage their financial planning. They know where they are now and where they want to be in the future. They are used to taking the time to evaluate their actions in the past and relate them to the achievements in their present. They also don't pretend. In my case, I lost more than I made when I tried investing in the stock market on my own years ago, and I had to decide to stop doing it altogether or to rely on the services of someone who was more experienced and passionate about it. I know I need help and appreciate others' expertise. In Mark's case, he began to realize that hanging out with people who were very generous in their spending did not help him achieve his dreams, so he reorganized his choices. He shifted his focus from "have to" to "want to," and he created a plan to restructure his lifestyle gradually so he could be more comfortable with himself. As he explored being more authentic, he was able to make better choices for his future and be less anxious about his present.

Wealthy people build a relationship between the past, the present, and the future. Understanding these relationships is energizing. You take action today to build your future by analyzing your past.

Wealthy people know that being poor is expensive: products and services usually have poorer quality; fees and interest raise costs; and time spent finding better values for money consumes time that could be used to generate more income.

Remember to have an emergency cushion. Wealthy people know that emergencies will not affect their finances greatly. This is the most important practical advice I can give a person who considers himself or herself poor. Create a safety cushion that sits in a risk-free, readily accessible form, only to be used in case of emergencies. Having that cushion saved me a lot of money when I was poor. On the few occasions I needed that cushion—a broken car, a medical emergency, an extra tax payment, a critical home repair, a move, a school trip—I did not have to rush to get some expensive money. If you don't already have one, building a safety cushion is the smartest thing you can do, right now. Having cash available to negotiate has shown me how important it is to be wealthy. Even when I had to borrow money to replace my car, I was able to make a good down payment and get a better deal. When that happened, I quickly rebuilt my emergency cushion by reducing my expenses, because I had started to notice how much cheaper being wealthy is.

A financial planner or your common sense will help you determine what suits you best. Having a safety cushion gives you peace of mind that allows you to enjoy your life more and take advantage of living in the present. For people who are struggling financially, nothing is sweeter than a safety cushion overflow. After that savings goal is reached, they can then indulge themselves briefly be- fore starting their plans to save money to be used for investments. The thought of living off your wealth and not your time is a strong motivator to keep you on the right track.

One last thing about the safety cushion and investing: when the cash that comes in is less than the cash that goes out, the wealth flow is negative. The difference is usually covered by some form of debt. If you need to rebalance your wealth flow, start by looking at how to reduce your outflow first and how to increase your inflow after that. If you don't have one, your first priority has to be to build a safety cushion; pay the minimum on your debt until you build a cushion you are happy with, and then start rebalancing your debt. There are many programs and systems to help you manage debt. However, there are also people who are ignorant, careless, or indifferent about your well-being. Remember that you choose with whom to work; they don't choose you. Be demanding and selective. Put yourself first.

Habit #7:
Complaining

Complaining

Anna complains that women are discriminated against.

Peter complains that black people are discriminated against.

Sophia complains about having parents who did not feed her properly.

John complains about having the wrong genes that make him fat.

Carolyn complains about having to wear children's clothing.

Mark complains about not finding a loving and smart partner.

Joan complains about having to do housekeeping chores.

Tom complains about living away from his children and having to pay so much in alimony.

Lisa complains about how you need to have "experience" to get a solid job.

Paul complains about the lack of opportunities he has because he has aged.

Unwealthy people spend precious time focusing on what is out of their control. As there is no possibility to change these circumstances, the feeling of helplessness sinks in.

Complaining

UNWEALTHY PEOPLE FEEL THAT LUCK has an extraordinary impact on their lives, and they focus on what is affecting them negatively. This creates a habit of self-pity that feeds into their low self-esteem and prevents them from thinking creatively and positively about how they manage their resources.

Complaining is quite dangerous because it kills hope. Without hope, we don't act; without action, we can't succeed or fail. Nothing happens, and the energy is lost or, worse, we become stagnant.

Each minute spent on sharing despair is a minute lost in thinking about opportunities, either discovering or creating them. A complaint about what is beyond your control is useless. We cannot control everything, but we can certainly control how we think and act.

As I was updating this edition, I caught pneumonia and ended up in a hospital. The place was filled with sick, grumpy people, like me. We were all complaining about the weather, medicine, health care, nurses, equipment, and food. We all know of an old lady who is a big complainer; well, here she was, lying in a bed next to me, complaining about everything. Sure enough, her phone didn't work, so I offered her my mobile phone, and she accepted only if she could pay me for the phone call. Although it was not necessary, I thought I would honor her dignity and accept payment. She gave me ten dollars and then complained to her son that the lady next to her was charging a fortune! It made me smile.

Complaining does not help ease discomfort or solve a problem. Used randomly, it causes rejection from others; if used frequently, it creates inertia. Rhonda Britten, in her book *Fearless Living*, offered venting out as an alternative to complaining. It is a natural reaction to rebel against what we don't like. She suggested we empty a half-filled glass instead of waiting for it to fill, so we can move on faster.

Take a walk instead of complaining. Vitus Dröscher wrote about rats' capacity to handle stress. When given an electric charge, rats that were not able to move at all developed higher stress—measured by the area of a stomach ulcer—than those who were allowed to move only one foot slightly. Since I read that, I have gone for a walk whenever I needed to complain. Instead of verbalizing my complaint, I took action to release the pressure. You can choose an activity that might help you release the frustration in a way that is not destructive. If you find yourself complaining often, it is time to find an alternative and use your time more wisely.

Let's look at Joan's case. She finds doing repetitive chores, especially household chores, boring. Her minutes are filled with mechanical tasks that deplete her energy. Every day, she complains about having to do it all again. She misses out on some of the wonders of life because she is busy complaining. She has become so good at it that when she meets with her friends, they compete for the worst complaint! However, sharing her misery does not make her feel better; rather, it leaves her convinced that life is not fair and that she doesn't have a chance, and it feeds into her other unwealthy habits. What is worse, nobody seems to have sympathy for her. She is more and more frustrated, and she feels more and more isolated. She wishes someone would understand her, but either they are too busy with their own complaints or they ignore her.

The vaccine against complaining is creativity. When you create, you forget about limitations. Write a poem, make a drawing, create a new step or dance, play a tune, whistle, invent, innovate. Find the time and space to create something; distract yourself from your complaining with your creativity. You will see how your complaining diminishes drastically.

Wealthy people find creative ways to live, manage their resources (time and money), and interact with others. More than feeling successful and finding new ways of doing things, thinking "outside of the box" serves as a way to nurture a feeling of self-esteem and uniqueness.

Creativity is liberating because when we create, there are no expectations, no status quo, and no end. When we are creating, we take each failure as a learning opportunity that can serve as a spring- board for creating bigger, bolder, higher, and more challenging situations. By focusing on how you solve problems or create a better future, you empower your own uniqueness. Children excel at creativity because they are not afraid to fail. You set yourself free to create when you are free to explore and be curious without expecting a result. When we get used to being creative, we get better and better at it. Creating something brings out our sense of usefulness to the world.

Joan could free up some time with better planning, find someone else to do chores, reinvent the way she and her family live, or simply begin a project that allows her brain to be active while she is working on repetitive tasks. She hasn't thought about using her frustration productively. A number of modern conveniences, including refrigerators, washing machines, ironing boards, vacuum cleaners, electricity, even plant genetics and agrochemicals that increased crop yields and reduced labor, were all made by people bored by repetitive actions.

When you create, you are free, you have fun; you feel active and useful, and you find ways to serve others, which in turn makes you more valuable and makes your life much more enjoyable. You never want to revert back to complaining because you are having fun.

Habit #8:
Comparing
Yourself
To Others

Comparing Yourself to Others

Anna thinks she is worse off than Joe because he got a new promotion.

Peter thinks he is better than his brother because he owns a Lexus.

Sophia thinks she is better than her sister because she is skinnier.

John thinks he is a worse salesman than Jerry because he is shorter.

Carolyn thinks she is better than her friends because she looks prettier.

Mark thinks he is better than most people because he exercises.

Joan thinks she is better than her friends because her house is always tidy.

Tom thinks he is worse off than his colleagues because he pays alimony.

Lisa thinks she is better than her co-workers because she has more energy.

Paul thinks he is wiser than his co-workers because he is older.

Unwealthy people look at those who are better or worse off than them- selves to evaluate their own progress in life. They always find someone smarter and wealthier who makes them feel insecure. They then judge others to reaffirm to themselves that they are not that bad.

Comparing Yourself to Others

UNWEALTHY PEOPLE COMPARE THEMSELVES TO OTHERS; they forget that the control of their lives lies in the way they think, feel, and act, from the inside out, not from the outside in.

Comparing ourselves with others is like handling a double-edged knife. There is no way to come out clean. Better yet, one must be extremely careful in handling comparisons. If you feel your circumstances have determined your outcomes—as they could have—you could be resentful if you feel you are worse off or arrogant and pedantic if you have outperformed others. Neither case is the best way to view your life, because it depends on the outcomes of others' lives, not on your own evolution, and because no matter how hard you try, you cannot control other people's outcomes.

When you focus on others, you forget how to evaluate your life and get used to measuring success externally instead of internally. That creates confusion and a feeling of helplessness, since, although sometimes you can influence others, you cannot control their lives.

When you look at your own journey, you get better results. You become stronger and more fulfilled when you think you are in control of your success, your happiness, and your life as a whole. You don't always control your circumstances, but you will always control one hundred percent of your attitude. That feeling is reassuring.

These days, we are more similar to each other and less like ourselves. Such standardization has done wonders for efficiency; thus, products and services have more competitive prices. Yet, it is a growing struggle for people to find a space that balances two conflicting forces: being unique and belonging to a group. Luckily, we have come to understand that as we begin to satisfy our basic needs, we tend to be freer to express our differences in ways that benefit diversity.

Carol Dweck's research on motivation is quite interesting. She highlights what I have called "the curse of genius." When gifted children are praised for their achievements, they lose the capacity to question themselves and accept rejection, challenges, and hardship. The praising becomes—in my words—a curse, as these children learn to be amazing, not because of their efforts, but as a matter of genetics, in which they played absolutely no part. If you feel that you are in any way superior to others, how do you dare to attempt the unknown or to learn and fail? The joy of life is in the journey, not in the destination. There is a certain emptiness in achieving milestones without great effort. Without challenges, we do not grow. We want to earn our successes. The empowerment of thinking that we can overcome challenges is rejuvenating.

Let's look at Tom's case. He feels uneasy about the arrangements he has made with his former spouse. He feels that the system has not helped him and that the law has unfairly treated a capable and professional person—his ex-wife—as someone who is incapable of supporting herself. He felt they were working as a team. The system failed to recognize that his hard work and determination were crucial for their financial prosperity and that during their marriage, many disagreements about spending patterns left him feeling stressed. With that in mind, he doubts he will ever be able to trust another person enough to share his life and dreams again for fear of being considered a walking bank.

Tom also thinks he is not as smart as other men because he did not get a good divorce settlement. He feels that he wasn't capable of standing up for himself. He gets annoyed every time he remembers how he had to find a rented place and live for months without the comforts he had worked so hard to achieve and how he had to manage his children's visits without access to toys and their beds or pillows. He still resents the time when he took his little daughter to the movies, and she did not have her favorite movie puppet. She cried through half of the movie. He feels he should have half of their toys at his place and be acknowledged for being an active father at school and after-school activities, and he wants to participate in selecting summer camps for them. He feels inadequate in managing his part of these expenses and fears any conversation about alimony with potential partners. Most of his friends don't have this problem. Because there will always be someone better off than Tom, he is missing out.

A brilliant student and an accomplished professional, Tom is no longer motivated to excel. Managing his firm has become quite stressful, and he doesn't want to increase his earnings because he feels part of whatever he earns will invariably go to satisfy someone else— his ex—who is not working toward the same goals. He never has enough money to spend on his children or to save for a retirement that will allow him to spend his time painting, a childhood passion. He feels he is caught in a trap, forced to do something that is no longer exciting, struggling to balance business and life, and wondering if he will ever find a partner with whom to spend his old age. He often wonders about his bad luck with his partners.

The vaccine against comparing oneself with others is self-awareness. When you look at your own life and realize how you create the life you live, you are in control, feel empowered to take action, think creatively, appreciate your efforts, and feel good about yourself. You create the life you want.

No matter what you are facing in life, you can always look back to find reassurance in decisions that were appropriate and humility in decisions that were wrong. Even if you are not happy with what you've accomplished so far, if you feel you are in control, you begin to plan, to make smart choices, and to learn from your mistakes and your successes.

We tend to think that failure is the opposite of success. It isn't. Both failure and success are the opposite of inaction. Deciding not to do anything is also a choice, and it is the worst one, by the way.

Doing nothing is worse than failing, because you don't even learn. When you take action, you inevitably put yourself at risk. Focusing on your journey allows you to evolve. When you stretch yourself in any direction in which you want to explore, you open up your life for enjoyment and wisdom. You make better decisions, and even when you fail, you gain a lesson. Tom can use his learning.

Wealthy people feel good about what they've done. They compare themselves within the situation in their own lives—not against the lives of others. Considering that we were pretty useless when we began living, chances are that we can find ways to feel happy about our accomplishments. Wealthy people enjoy the journey, each destination being a step that has a new path forward. In the process, they feel free to rejoice in their successes, make corrections, learn, and even apologize. They don't need to be perfect, as they are not comparing themselves to anyone. Perfection is irrelevant.

We don't need to be better than anybody else; we need to be better than ourselves.

Habit #9: Measuring your Worth by What you Own

Measuring your Worth by What you Own

Anna thinks she will be wealthy if she can have half a million dollars.

Peter thinks he will be wealthy if he can have a million dollars.

Sophia thinks she will be wealthy if she can have a million dollars.

John thinks he will be wealthy if he can have half a million dollars.

Carolyn thinks she will be wealthy if she can have a million dollars.

Mark thinks he will be wealthy if he can have three million dollars.

Joan thinks she will be wealthy if she can have a million dollars.

Tom thinks he will be wealthy if he can have ten million dollars.

Lisa thinks she will be wealthy if she can have five million dollars.

Paul thinks he will be wealthy if he can have a million dollars.

Unwealthy people think that wealth is only a matter of money; they over- look other resources. Money is just part of wealth. We like it because it is an objective measurement, making it easy to draw conclusions and evaluate alternatives. The most valuable resource we have is our time, not our money. It is the only limiting factor, and we never know when it will cease to exist.

Measuring your Worth by What you Own

MONEY IS AN ILLUSION. We may think we like money, but what we really like is what we can do with money. Intuitively, we prefer to think more about wealth than about money, because we know that wealth is a far wider concept. Money is a way of keeping score, mainly because we live in a society where money has become an objective measurement. Rich people have a lot of money; wealthy people have a positive flow of resources. The real measure of wealth is the flow of resources. When we think about resources instead of money, we create and discover new opportunities. It is what we expect to do with money that empowers us to have more.

There are many hidden costs and benefits that can help us balance the flow of resources in a way that works best for us. When we realize that our circumstances play a role in our wealth, we begin to look at money in a more practical way. When we limit our thoughts to money alone, we fail to see how we can creatively use the other resources we might have available, such as friendships, time, knowledge, and other assets. For example, I once lived in a very luxurious house because the owners traveled to France for two years to study. What I paid to live there did not amount even to half of the market value of the rent, but my living there allowed the owners to save on storage and other costs, and it allowed me to enjoy an exquisite home.

Money follows opportunities. When I was managing an investment fund, I realized that there were alternatives to money. I called that "capital-less funding." It is a whole new method of funding in which entrepreneurs find natural collaborators. For example, one of my clients needed funds to finalize the development of some software. We negotiated an agreement with a company that could integrate the software with its products. The company paid for the development in exchange for a customized version and got an extraordinary competitive advantage. Not only did they offer to pay an upfront amount, but they also put my client in touch with a programming company that had given them excellent results. Besides saving money, my client saved the time that would have been needed to raise funds, train and pay a salesperson, and find the appropriate software company to finalize their services on time.

When we measure wealth only with money, we leave out many other resources. There are several hidden costs and benefits. Some costs are easy to measure, such as fees, cost of time, and interest rates. Others, such as costs to the environment, health, and well-being, are more difficult to determine. Many people, for example, are prepared to pay more for produce that is grown closer to where they live, in an organic way, using fair-trade agreements, and so on. People do care.

Unwealthy people think about money, not resources. Because they are fixated on money, they fail to evaluate benefits beyond money.

Thinking about money as wealth is the same as equating price and value. Savvy marketers know that value and price are not interchangeable. We know that intuitively, too. Even a standard product like water has different values under different circumstances. Marketers use these differences very well. Think about how much you would value water at a friend's home, at an airport, on a deserted island, or at a high-end spa; think about how much you would pay too.

Let's look at Paul's case. He jokes that instead of living in the "golden years," he has entered the "rotten age." He had high expectations about wealth and freedom and resents having to work to support his lifestyle. His sense of adventure makes him overspend on gadgets for hobbies, sports, and other activities that do not bring him real joy and deplete his resources.

Paul could be considered wealthy by many people. He has both savings and investments, yet when he started to keep track of the time he spent enjoying himself and the time he felt worried, he saw a different picture. He also evaluated what money could buy him. His tendency to jump from one sport to another has made a big dent in his finances. He has purchased a racecar, a horse, and a small plane. He has expensive tastes, and even though he can afford these expensive items, the joy he gets from exploring and learning new sports is not worth the time he spends worrying about paying for them, keeping up with races and competitions and maintaining a good performance.

Paul's need for money is self-imposed and largely based on his need to show others how rich he is. He does not need a car he has not raced in a year. Nor does he need to maintain a horse he has long since stopped enjoying. He also does not need the yacht he is considering purchasing.

Paul could be considered a wealthy person, but he thinks more about what he needs to do than what he wants to do. To Paul, having more money means spending more money, and he calculates his wealth as the value of his assets. These assets do not contribute to his wealth; on the contrary, they deplete it.

Robert Kiyosaki's famous book *Rich Dad, Poor Dad* highlights one of the most valuable lessons about wealth, which is that assets create income. I take it one step further and assert that assets need to create rewards. In other words, you can enjoy the home of your dreams even if it does not create income for you as long as your emotional rewards are higher than your emotional costs. When you realize that the value of your resources is larger than their monetary value, you make better decisions. These decisions allow you to be true to yourself and reflect your unique set of values. Marketers know this, and the overflow of advertisements to convince you that life is much better with this or that product can create confusion. The perceived values are inside of you and are unique to each individual. Look inward to find them.

Another author, Barry Schwartz, in his book *The Paradox of Choice*, explains how having many choices makes selection harder and overwhelms our capacity to take action. With fewer choices, people make more purchases. Furthermore, people are happier with fewer choices. We are getting used to having services and products that we don't value; thus, our time is spent on instant gratification because of the profusion of messages.

Our friend Paul went for a long walk after we evaluated his time spent in joy versus worry. He did not stop by the gym; he just walked and lost himself in his surroundings. He noticed the smell of the street, the noisy road, that there were no birds. He began counting the trees only to realize that he was trying to find the tallest—a competitive trait, he thought. He made a plan to go fishing, with the simplest rod he could take, but, as it turned out, he never went. The fishing store was great, and he did some research on the Internet to find the best deals and the best brands. But instead of purchasing that simple rod, he made a list of how he used his income and gradually started to shift from spending to saving and sold off the assets that were not providing him either joy or income.

The vaccine against measuring wealth with money is to value our joyful time. Wealthy people don't have more money. They have enough because they don't feel the need to have more. Our most limiting factor in life is time, not wealth. When we learn to balance our lives in ways that give us time to enjoy, to learn, to help others, we are wealthy. When we realize that we can have a great time without spending money, money becomes secondary to happiness.

When we become aware that we are needed and set aside time to volunteer for a cause that is meaningful to us, we realize how wealthy we really are.

Wealthy people don't "need" money; instead, they attract it. It's not that they want to be poor or think that living with less money is spiritual in any way. Wealthy people have broken the ties between success and money and wealth and money. Success is being able to do what you are absolutely passionate about doing; being wealthy is having more resources than you need because you created them. Assets don't measure wealth; value does. Your assets should build your wealth in terms of fulfillment and/or income. They should give you energy, not worries. Build up your assets accordingly.

When you break the tie between wealth and money, you learn to enjoy your life whether or not you have money. When money becomes irrelevant to your happiness, you make better choices because they are based on what you want to do, not on what you have to do or what you think others want you to do.

Habit #10: Isolating Yourself from Your Family

Isolating Yourself from Your Family

Anna doesn't talk to her family; they are all too weird.

Peter doesn't keep in touch with his relatives; they are all losers.

Sophia doesn't see her family; they never supported her.

John doesn't like his family; they are paranoid, aggressive, and sour.

Carolyn doesn't talk to her mother; she verbally abused her few years ago.

Mark hasn't seen his family in decades; they are too selfish.

Joan doesn't get along with her siblings; they always ask for money.

Tom hates his annual visit to his parents; he has nothing to tell them.

Lisa doesn't have the strength to deal with her strong-willed parents and siblings.

Paul doesn't connect with anybody in his family; he was a bit wild in his youth and prefers not to be reminded of that.

Unwealthy people can't accept their less-than-perfect relatives, and they become isolated and unhealthily selfish. They consider their family members to be unsupportive, difficult, or embarrassing.

Isolating Yourself from Your Family

THE RELATIONSHIP BETWEEN FAMILY AND WEALTH is a very interesting one. Families are the best connectors to our essence.

They don't define us, but the way we deal with our family does define us. Childhood is a free and spontaneous time in our lives. Staying connected with our ties from childhood helps us focus on our goals and values. Maurice Nicoll recorded in his *Commentaries* Gurdjieff's notion that after the authenticity of our early years, we enter a stage of confusion about who we are, what we want, and what our purpose is in life. Later in life, we reach an age when our future no longer dominates our thinking and we begin to reconcile with our past to become who we were really meant to be. That is, of course, if we are lucky enough to live that long.

That is why families are so important. They help us tie the knots between our past and our present. Families are great sources of inspiration, tension, growth, love, and compassion. Because we do not choose our relatives, they provide a great opportunity to give, request, test, reject, go beyond our boundaries, explore who we are, inspire, leave a legacy, and accept or tolerate differences. We should be profoundly grateful and appreciative of our family in the most expanded concept. Unwealthy people see their family as a matter of shame, gossip, and frustration.

Let's look at Lisa's case. She resents the fact that her parents and siblings always have an opinion about her life. She is apprehensive about spending holidays with her family because their remarks make her feel uncomfortable. She dislikes that aspect of her visits immensely. "As if they were perfect," is her natural response to their comments. Her brother is not able to hold a steady job, and her sister is a snob who brags about her vegetarianism and volunteering somewhere in Asia.

Her father thinks Lisa neglects her parents and should spend more time visiting. Her mother complains about her father continually. Once Lisa visited to celebrate a promotion, only to hear the comment, "Don't fly too high, so the fall doesn't hurt that much. You will always be you." Lisa sees with a mixture of envy and sadness how some of her friends have supportive parents. She can't imagine her mother saying, "We are so proud of you." She doesn't re- member ever getting a call from her parents. When she moved last, her family offered to come see the new house "after you are done unpacking." She has withdrawn from her family to the extent that she feels a large weight upon her when holidays are approaching. She does not care for them anymore.

When she visits, Lisa spends beyond her means to bring presents. She does not enjoy the hours spent shopping online to find the perfect gifts for her relatives. In the process, she finds things that she likes and becomes even more irritable because she is not able to indulge herself since she "has to" take presents to her relatives. To show her parents that she is successful, she takes them out to expensive restaurants and invites them to nearby casinos. Then she spends the next three months struggling to meet her own financial commitments.

The vaccine against isolating yourself from your family is acceptance.

Nothing is more rewarding than feeling love for those who are related to you and (I hope) were there for you when you were growing up and whom you've been with as they were growing up.

Families provide a great test tank for all emotions. We judge our relatives more critically for two reasons: they are tied to us forever, and we feel that they represent us. Most of us prefer our friends to our relatives. It is easier to relate to someone when you know that you can break the relationship.

The bond we have with our family does not dissolve easily. My grandfather used to say, "Blood does not turn into water," meaning that family bonds are unbreakable. Some of my relatives have put that saying to the test many times, providing great stories in the process.

Family supports our sense of belonging to a group. Because of that, we tend to internalize the successes and failures of our relatives, and we want all of them to be perfect. When I hear some- one make a comment on a less-than-desirable personality trait of a relative, almost inevitably, an explanation is added: that trait comes from the "other" side of the family.

Relatives provide an exceptional opportunity to accept diversity. I had difficult times both with my mother when I was growing up and with my daughter when she was growing up. I wanted them both to be perfect. It was my daughter who pointed out the issue about my desire to have a perfect family during an argument we were having. She kept telling me that our differences were not about me but about her need to discover who she was. After several at-tempts to reach an agreement and as the energy level was increasing, she raised her voice and yelled, "Because you are not the perfect mother and I am not the perfect daughter!" Then it all made sense to me. I wanted a perfect family. What a waste of opportunities! When my family is not up to my standards, I lose patience. It reflects badly on me to have relatives who are not like the fairy-tale characters I would like them to be. If I can't love them as they are and respect their evolution in life, their capacity to overcome their challenges, and their freedom to fail, how can I learn and under- stand others outside of my family? And what are my expectations from my relatives in my times of worry, when I am feeling weak, when I am failing, or when I experience success?

It is very easy to have friends because we pick them. Even better, we can dispose of friends, which give relationships a healthy fragility. We can even break marriages that we once supposed would last forever. We are so concerned with our relatives' imperfections that we can't face them when we ourselves are the ones making mistakes. Chances are they are going to be as supportive to us as we are to them. No wonder.

One of my most beautiful lessons about relationships came through my first mother-in-law. She is one of those gifted people who can always find a way to comfort you and make you feel good, loved, and cared for. I was a couple of weeks from having my first child when our dog was stolen. I followed a trail to the city where my in-laws lived and convinced my husband to go to the slums where I knew our dog was. We arrived late at night as my in-laws were going to bed. As we explained what we wanted to do, she tried to convince us to stay. Frustrated, emotional, and hurt, I told her, "It is none of your business."

She calmly replied, "Of course it is; I love you, and I care for you." When years later I apologized, she simply replied that there was no need for apologies. Her level of acceptance was remarkable. Everybody felt great in her company.

Wealthy people understand their role in promoting healthy family ties. They are active participants in sustaining and nurturing family members, not out of pity or arrogance, but out of love. Wealthy people work on their differences, show compassion toward other family members' weaknesses, and get inspired by other family members' greatness.

David Pelzer, victim of one of the worst cases of child abuse in the United States, gives us a great inspiration about how to turn complex families into learning opportunities. His books and presentations about overcoming these challenges are proof that one can turn very difficult situations into something positive.

Wealthy people are not blind to challenges in family relationships; instead, they use their creativity to foster and create solutions. They value honest communication with their relatives, encourage reciprocity, expect help, offer help, and learn. They don't want to miss being there for the new generations, either. Having that sense of value and belonging empowers people within a close, intimate circle, which in turn builds confidence. Confident people make better decisions.

Wealthy people don't have better families; they work on having better families and healthy family ties.

My Habit-Changing System

Now that you have put on your glasses and can see these ten unwealthy habits, make a plan to change those you wish to. There is no easy way to change a habit, and there is no universal way that applies to everybody. More than complexity, the best methods to change habits involve consistency. Changing a habit is better than making them disappear. Plan that change. If you are concerned about your wealth and have found that you share some of the challenges or worries represented in our cases, it is time to take action.

My Habit-Changing System

I HAVE MY OWN SYSTEM FOR CHANGING HABITS. I modified it from a system of a friend who tried to stop smoking in the seventies.

The system begins with a focus on awareness. Just that. We don't want to change anything, only heighten our awareness. Habits are difficult to change because they can be invisible to us. By becoming aware of them, we make our habits real.

The next phase is to plan the change we want. Habits are easier to substitute than to eliminate, and we are better prepared to make this substitution if we know what do we want instead.

The final phase is the consistent replacement of a habit for another behavior. We finish by completely substituting an unwanted habit with a desired one. As I mentioned initially, habits are invisible. We have completely substituted one habit for another when we forget about the new habit.

Here are the steps:

1. Know your habit.
2. Define the change.
3. Implement the change; focus on the first change and then on increasing the changing rate.
4. Replace the old habit with your new habit.

Let's see the system in detail:

1. **Know your habit**: Choose a habit you want to change. Study it like an advanced course in human behavior: When does it happen? What triggers it? How do you feel before, during, and after? Study your habit to become more aware of it, not just to modify it, and not to judge yourself or to feel bad about it. Take the time to know the circumstances that lead up to your behavior. Reflect on what happens, yet block any negative feeling about this particular habit. Just be curious and try to describe the situation. Make notes at the end of the day. If your friends can help make external observations, ask them to recall what your behavior is and what leads you to it. Create a pattern for the habit you want to change.

2. **Define the change**: the best way to handle a negative or unwanted habit is by changing it not by eliminating it. In this sense, instead of thinking of the habit as a problem, we can achieve more effective and faster results if we focus on the solution. Define what your alternative is. As you noticed through the vaccines suggested, we do not get rid of the habit when we eliminate it or when we try the opposite of a habit. For example, to change the habit of complaining, it is very difficult to take the path of elimination. To 'stop complaining' is too vague to be able to take action. To do the opposite, finding a positive side of a complaint to praise it, is irrational. Worse even, to praise what we dislike is unauthentic and unnatural and disconnects us from our true feelings, after all, we are complaining because we are not happy. We can't like what we don't want. It is much easier and healthier to take a different path than the opposite. We can make a conscious decision to find something we are grateful for, even if it is not related to what we are complaining about. If we get used to be grateful, for what we are truly grateful, we are consciously reshaping the way our thoughts and emotions are intertwined, therefore, easing making changes in the habit of complaining.

3. **Initiate and strengthen change**: start by focusing on your first change. Remember that the first step is the hardest, habits put us on automatic and are very difficult to change initially. First, you will find your habit after it happens, then during it, until you can consciously grasp the pre-habit stage and are able to take action.

Our emotions and thoughts connect automatically by repetition, and changing that path can be energetically costly. We need to use our conscience, our reasoning, to interfere. In the case of animals, conditioning – a treat or a punishment- can change habits. You can use conditioning externally by asking friends to provide a treat or punishment or by using a self-regulating mechanism. You can also create a reminder and get used to reading it. That way, you are preparing a new pathway. Remember that change is possible, and that the energy required for change diminishes with every replacement of an unwanted habit for a wanted one. Still, relapses are to be expected.

After the initial change, the next focus is on increasing the conversion rate. Do you feel better? Can you celebrate or share that you were able to change a habit? You can strengthen your sense of achievement through a reward system. If you can discuss it, that is when support groups come handy! Look for external rewards, and value your effort. Do not expect to change a behavior completely at once but to make one change at a time. If you fall back, recommit. This is part of the process of change. Simple as that.

4. **Forget the old habit**: If you have managed to replace a habit for another more beneficial habit, you will forget about it, unless someone else points out that you have changed or if you consciously want to look back and help another person change a habit.

My last words in this book relate to your prosperity. I wrote this book thinking that there are more efficient ways of achieving our objectives. I hope these notes will help you manage the anchors or breaks that are holding you back, so you can have a fuller life, not only for you but for all of us... Because we need the best in all of us.

When we are prosperous, the money is not so important in our lives, and we have more freedom to enjoy life and share our prosperity with others. When we are wealthy can understand that nobody has to lose for us to win, our communities thrive and we build a better world. It all sounds good but it only works if we realize that, in the middle of prosperity there is one person: You. Prosperity flows from inside out, like success and happiness, is a decision, not an outcome.

Finally I would like to invite you to share your observations with us: If you have benefited from this book, if you have some suggestions, or if you simply want to connect, please contact us on our site www.thetenunwealthyhabits.com. You can also leave a comment on www.amazon.com or find us online. We are always interested in making this world a better world, and we know we cannot do it without help.

Here's to your prosperity.

Alicia Castillo Holley
www.thetenunwealthyhabits.com

Recommended Reading

Rhonda Britten. *Fearless Living*, 2002. ISBN-13: 978-0399527531

Castillo Holley, Alicia. 2008. *Falling in Love with Your Life*, 2008. ISBN-13: 978-0980396409

Csikszentmihalyi, Mihaly. *Flow: Psychology of Optimal Experiences*, 2008. ISBN-13: 978-0061339202

Dweck, Carol. *Mindset: The New Psychology of Success*, 2007. ISBN-13: 978-0345472328

Klein, Stefan. *The Science of Happiness*, 2006. ISBN-13: 978-1569243282
Kiyosaki, Robert. *Rich Dad, Poor Dad*, 2000. ASIN: B000P13RVS
Orman, Suze. *The Road to Wealth*, 2008. ISBN-13: 978-1594489822

Pelzer, David. *A Child Called "It"*, 1995. ISBN-13: 978-1558743663

Schwartz, Barry. *The Paradox of Choice*, 2005. ISBN-13: 978-0060005696

www.ingramcontent.com/pod-product-compliance
Lightning Source LLC
Chambersburg PA
CBHW060147200526
45165CB00023B/983